D1030924

WORDS
TO SAY
THANK YOU

WORDS
TO SAY
THANK YOU

COMPILED BY SARAH HOGGETT

DESIGN BY DAVID FORDHAM

CICO BOOKS
LONDON NEW YORK

First published in 2007 by CICO BOOKS
An imprint of
Ryland Peters & Small
20–21 Jockey's Fields   519 Broadway, 5th Floor
London WC1R 4BW   New York, NY 10012

10 9 8 7 6 5 4 3 2 1

A CIP catalog record for this book is available from the Library of Congress
and the British Library.

US ISBN-13: 978 1 904991 69 4
US ISBN-10: 1 904991 69 6

UK ISBN-13: 978 1 904991 68 7
UK ISBN-10: 1 904991 68 8

Printed in China

Designer: David Fordham

CONTENTS

INTRODUCTION

In our hectic lives, it can be all too easy to take things for granted and forget just how much we have to be thankful for: the love of our family, the support of our friends, and the sheer beauty of the world around us. And it's even easier to forget to express our thanks.

WORDS TO SAY THANK YOU contains over 60 memorable quotations from the ancient world to the present day, from poets and philosophers to stars of the silver screen. There are all kinds of ways in which you can use them. Inscribe them in homemade greetings cards or on a scrapbook layout commemorating a special occasion. Pin your favorites to your office noticeboard, where they will serve as a daily reminder to acknowledge and be grateful for all the good things in your life. Text or e-mail them to your friends and family. Or simply dip into this book from time to time and take inspiration from what you find.

So open your eyes. Repay a friend's (or a stranger's) kindnesses with a few words of gratitude. Rejoice in the love of your partner and family. Recapture the sense of wonder that was yours as a child and learn again to gaze in awe at the miracles of nature, from a budding leaf in your back yard to a multicolored rainbow in the sky.

Give thanks for all the good things in your life—and remember: in the words of Mother Teresa of Calcutta,

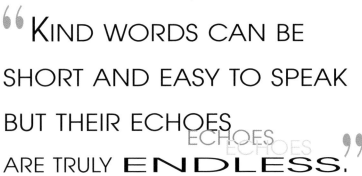

" KIND WORDS CAN BE SHORT AND EASY TO SPEAK BUT THEIR ECHOES ARE TRULY ENDLESS. "

"SWIFT GRATITUDE IS THE SWEETEST."

Greek proverb

THANK YOU, MY FRIEND

"The **only** way to have a friend is to **be one**."

" IF I DON'T HAVE FRIENDS, THEN

I AIN'T GOT NOTHIN. "

Billie Holiday (1915–1959)

" Forsake not an *old* friend; for the **new** is not comparable to him: a **new** friend is as **new** wine; when it is *old*, thou shalt drink it with PLEASURE. **"**

Bible, Ecclesiasticus, 9:10

"A FRIEND IS ONE TO WHOM ONE MAY POUR OUT ALL THE CONTENTS OF ONE'S HEART, CHAFF AND GRAIN ALIKE, KNOWING THAT THE GENTLEST OF HANDS WILL KEEP WHAT IS WORTH KEEPING AND, WITH A BREATH OF KINDNESS, BLOW THE REST AWAY."

Arab Proverb

"WE ARE FRIENDS AND
I DO LIKE TO PASS THE DAY
WITH YOU IN SERIOUS AND
INCONSEQUENTIAL CHATTER.

I WOULDN'T MIND WASHING
UP BESIDE YOU, DUSTING
BESIDE YOU, READING THE
ВАСК HALF OF THE PAPER
WHILE YOU READ THE FRONT.

WE ARE FRIENDS AND I WOULD
MISS YOU, DO MISS YOU AND
THINK OF YOU VERY OFTEN."

Jeanette Winterson (1959–)

"A friend is a gift
you give yourself."

Robert Louis Stevenson (1850–1894)

**Friendship is the
only cement that
will ever hold
the world
together."**

Woodrow Wilson (1856–1924)

" *I WANT TO BE YOUR FRIEND*
FOR EVER AND EVER WITHOUT BREAK OR DECAY.

When the hills are all flat,
And the rivers are all dry,
When it lightens and thunders in winter,
When it rains and snows in summer,
When Heaven and Earth mingle—
NOT TILL THEN WILL I PART FROM YOU. "

Anon, 1st century CE, translated from Chinese by Arthur Waley

"A TRUE FRIEND IS THE **GREATEST** OF ALL BLESSINGS, & THE ONE THAT WE TAKE THE **LEAST** CARE OF ALL TO ACQUIRE."

François de la Rochefoucauld (1613–1680)

" OF ALL THE THINGS WHICH *WISDOM* PROVIDES TO MAKE LIFE ENTIRELY HAPPY, MUCH THE GREATEST IS THE *POSSESSION OF FRIENDSHIP*. "

Epicurus (341–270 BCE)

LET'S COUNT OUR BLESSINGS

> "AN EARLY-MORNING WALK IS A *blessing* FOR THE WHOLE DAY."

Henry David Thoreau (1817–1862)

> "**HUMOR** IS MANKIND'S **GREATEST** BLESSING."

Mark Twain (1835–1910)

"REFLECT UPON YOUR PRESENT BLESSINGS, OF WHICH EVERY MAN HAS PLENTY; NOT ON YOUR PAST MISFORTUNES, OF WHICH ALL MEN HAVE SOME."

Charles Dickens (1812–1870)

"Count your JOYS instead of your WOES; Count your FRIENDS instead of your FOES."

Irish proverb

"DO NOT SPOIL WHAT YOU HAVE BY DESIRING WHAT YOU HAVE NOT;

but remember that

WHAT YOU NOW HAVE WAS ONCE AMONG THE THINGS YOU ONLY HOPED FOR."

Epicurus (341–270 BCE)

" Whatever I am offered in devotion with a pure heart—

a leaf, a flower, fruit, or water

—I accept with joy. "

The Bhagavadgita

"LET US RISE UP AND BE THANKFUL,

*for if we didn't learn a **LOT** today, at LEAST we learned a LITTLE, and if we didn't learn a LITTLE, at LEAST we didn't get sick, and if we got sick, at LEAST we didn't die;*

SO, LET US ALL BE THANKFUL."

Buddha, Prince Gautama Siddhartha (563–483 BCE)

"OF THE *BLESSINGS* SET BEFORE YOU MAKE YOUR CHOICE, AND BE *CONTENT*."

Samuel Johnson (1709–1784)

THANKS
FOR THE
GIFT OF LOVE

"Many waters cannot quench **love**,

Bible, Song of Solomon, 8:7

neither can floods drown *it*."

"WHAT DOES LOVE LOOK LIKE?

IT HAS THE HANDS TO HELP OTHERS. IT HAS THE FEET TO HASTEN TO THE POOR AND NEEDY. IT HAS EYES TO SEE MISERY AND WANT. IT HAS THE EARS TO HEAR THE SIGHS AND SORROWS OF MEN.

THAT IS WHAT LOVE LOOKS LIKE."

Saint Augustine (d. 603)

" KEEP LOVE IN YOUR HEART.
A LIFE WITHOUT IT IS LIKE
A SUNLESS GARDEN WHEN
THE FLOWERS ARE DEAD. "

Oscar Wilde (1854–1900)

" GIVE ME A KISS, AND TO THAT KISS A SCORE;
1 20

THEN TO THAT TWENTY, ADD A HUNDRED MORE:
20 100

A THOUSAND TO THAT HUNDRED: SO KISS ON,
1,000 100

TO MAKE THAT THOUSAND UP A MILLION.
1,000 1,000.000

TREBLE THAT MILLION, AND WHEN THAT IS DONE,
3,000.000

LET'S KISS AFRESH, AS WHEN WE FIRST BEGUN. "
1

Robert Herrick (1591–1674),
'To Anthea: Ah, My Anthea!'

"AT THE TOUCH OF LOVE, EVERYONE BECOMES A POET."

Plato (427–347 BCE)

"Come live with me, and be my love,
And we will some new pleasures prove,
Of golden sands, and crystal brooks,
With silken lines, and silver hooks."

John Donne 'The Bait' (1573–1611)

" As soon go kindle fire with snow, as seek to quench the fire of love with words. "

William Shakespeare (1564–1616)

"WHERE THERE IS LOVE THERE IS LIFE."

Mahatma Gandhi (1869–1948)

"LIFE *without* LOVE is like a tree *without* BLOSSOMS OR FRUIT."

Kahlil Gibran (1883–1931)

" LIFE *is the* flower for which **LOVE** *is the* honey. **"**

Victor Hugo (1802–1885)

"HOW DO I LOVE THEE? LET ME COUNT THE WAYS.

I LOVE THEE TO THE DEPTH AND breadth AND HEIGHT MY SOUL CAN REACH. "

Elizabeth Barrett Browning (1806–1861)

IT'S
A
WONDERFUL
WORLD

"If we could **SEE** the miracle of **A SINGLE FLOWER** clearly, **OUR WHOLE LIFE WOULD CHANGE**."

Buddha, Prince Gautama Siddhartha (563–483 BCE)

"CONSIDER THE LILIES OF THE FIELD, HOW THEY GROW; THEY TOIL NOT, NEITHER DO THEY SPIN : AND YET I SAY UNTO YOU, THAT EVEN SOLOMON IN ALL HIS GLORY WAS NOT ARRAYED LIKE ONE OF THESE."

Bible, Matthew, 6:28-29

"

PEOPLE USUALLY CONSIDER WALKING ON WATER OR IN THIN AIR *A MIRACLE*.

BUT I THINK *THE REAL MIRACLE* IS NOT TO WALK EITHER ON WATER OR IN THIN AIR, BUT TO WALK ON EARTH.

Thich Nhat Hanh (1926–)

EVERY DAY WE ARE ENGAGED IN *A MIRACLE* WHICH WE DON'T EVEN RECOGNIZE: A BLUE SKY, WHITE CLOUDS, GREEN LEAVES, THE BLACK, CURIOUS EYES OF A CHILD—OUR OWN TWO EYES. ALL IS *A MIRACLE*. **"**

> " *A* thing of beauty is a joy
> for ever:
> Its loveliness increases;
> It will never pass into
> nothingness;
> But still will keep a bower quiet
> for us,
> And a sleep full of sweet
> dreams,
> And health, and quiet
> breathing... "

John Keats *Endymion* (1795–1821)

"NOTHING IS MORE BEAUTIFUL THAN THE LOVELINESS OF THE WOODS BEFORE SUNRISE."

George Washington Carver (1864–1943)

"Who can paint Like Nature? Can imagination boast, Amid its gay creation, hues like hers?"

James Thomson 'Spring', *The Seasons* (1700–1748)

66 All the wild world is beautiful, and it matters but little where we go, to **highlands** or **lowlands**, woods or plains, on the sea or land or **down** among the crystals of waves or **high** in a balloon in the sky; through all the climates, hot or cold, storms and calms, everywhere and always we are in God's eternal beauty and love. So universally true is this, the spot where we chance to be always seems the best. **99**

John Muir (1838–1914)

"THE
SUN,
WITH ALL THOSE
PLANETS REVOLVING
AROUND IT & DEPENDENT
UPON IT, CAN STILL
RIPEN A BUNCH OF GRAPES
AS IF IT HAD NOTHING
ELSE IN THE UNIVERSE
TO DO."

Galileo (1564–1642)

" *I believe a leaf of grass is no less than the journey-work of the stars.* **"**

Walt Whitman (1819–1892)

"

MY HEART LEAPS UP WHEN I BEHOLD A

RAINBOW

IN THE SKY.

"

William Wordsworth (1770–1850)

66

i thank You God for most this amazing

day: for the ^{l}e$_a$p$_i$^{n}g greenly spirits of trees

and a blue true dream of sky; and for everything

which is natural which is infinite which is yes

e.e. cummings (1894–1962)

99

46

THANK YOU
FROM THE
SOUL

" No duty is more urgent than that of returning thanks. "

Saint Ambrose (340–397)

"GRATITUDE IS NOT ONLY THE GREATEST OF VIRTUES, BUT THE PARENT OF ALL OTHERS."

Marcus Tullius Cicero (106–43 BCE)

" LET US BE GRATEFUL TO PEOPLE WHO MAKE US HAPPY; THEY ARE THE *charming* GARDENERS WHO MAKE OUR SOULS BLOSSOM. "

Marcel Proust (1871–1922)

"GRATITUDE IS THE FAIREST BLOSSOM WHICH SPRINGS FROM THE SOUL."

Henry Ward Beecher (1813–1887)

66 As we express our

GRATITUDE,

WE MUST NEVER FORGET THAT

THE HIGHEST APPRECIATION IS

NOT TO UTTER WORDS, BUT TO

LIVE BY THEM. 99

John Fitzgerald Kennedy (1917–1963)

"THOU WHO HAST GIVEN ME SO MUCH, GIVE ME ONE THING MORE: A GRATEFUL HEART."

George Herbert (1593–1633)

"IF THE **ONLY PRAYER** YOU SAID IN **YOUR WHOLE LIFE** WAS, **'THANK YOU'**, THAT WOULD SUFFICE."

Meister Eckhart (1260–1327)

THANK YOU
FOR
MY FAMILY

"Of all nature's gifts to the human race, what is **sweeter** to a man than his children?"

Marcus Tullius Cicero (106–43 BCE)

"IT IS NOT FLESH & BLOOD *BUT THE* HE♥RT WHICH MAKES US FATHERS & SONS."

Friedrich von Schiller (1759–1805)

"WE NEVER KNOW THE LOVE OF OUR PARENTS FOR US

Henry Ward Beecher (1813–1887)

TILL WE HAVE BECOME PARENTS."

"What *do* girls do who haven't any mothers to help them through their troubles?"

Louisa May Alcott (1832–1888)

"Life began with WAKING up & loving my mother's face."

George Eliot (1819–1880)

"The HEART of a mother is a DEEP abyss at the

Honoré de Balzac (1799–1850)

B O T T O M

of which you will always find forgiveness."

"MOTHER: THE MOST BEAUTIFUL WORD ON THE LIPS OF MANKIND."

Kahlil Gibran (1883–1931)

SOURCES AND ACKNOWLEDGMENTS

The publishers are grateful for permission to reproduce extracts from works in copyright.

p. 14 Jeanette Winterson: From *Written on the Body* by Jeanette Winterson, published by Jonathan Cape. Reprinted by permission of Jeanette Winterson and The Random House Group Ltd.

p. 39 Thich Nhat Hanh: *From The Miracle of Mindfulness* by Thich Nhat Hanh, published by Rider. Reprinted by permission of The Random House Group Ltd.

p. 46 E. E. Cummings: reprinted from *Complete Poems 1904–1962*, by E.E. Cummings, edited by George J. Firmage, by permission of W.W. Norton & Company. Copyright © 1991 by the Trustees for the E.E. Cummings Trust and George James Firmage.

Every effort has been made to contact copyright holders and acknowledge sources, but the publishers would be glad to hear of any omissions.

INDEX
of
AUTHORS